DINOSAUR PROFILES

BRACHIOSAURUS

Titles in the Dinosaur Profiles series include:

Brachiosaurus

Caudipteryx

Deinonychus

Edmontosaurus

Scipionyx

Stegosaurus

Triceratops

Tyrannosaurus

DINOSAUR PROFILES

BRACHIOSAURUS

CONTRA COSTA COUNTY LIBRARY

Text by Fabio Marco Dalla Vecchia
Illustrations by Leonello Calvetti and Luca Massini

BLACKBIRCH®
PRESS

THOMSON
GALE

San Diego • Detroit • New York • San Francisco • Cleveland • New Haven, Conn. • Waterville, Maine • London • Munich

Copyright © 2003 by Andrea Dué s.r.l., Florence, Italy.

Published in 2004 in North America by Blackbirch Press. Blackbirch Press is an imprint of Thomson Gale, a part of the Thomson Corporation.

Thomson is a trademark and Gale [and Blackbirch Press] are registered trademarks used herein under license.

For more information, contact
The Gale Group, Inc.
27500 Drake Rd.
Farmington Hills, MI 48331-3535
Or you can visit our Internet site at http://www.gale.com

Computer illustrations 3D and 2D: Leonello Calvetti and Luca Massini

Photographs: pages 22–23 P. Morris/Ardea London; page 23 François Gohier/Ardea London

LIBRARY OF CONGRESS CATALOGING-IN-PUBLICATION DATA

Dalla Vecchia, Fabio Marco.
  Brachiosaurus / text by Fabio Marco Dalla Vecchia; illustrations by Leonello Calvetti and Luca Massini.
     p. cm. — (Dinosaur profiles)
  Includes bibliographical references and index.
  ISBN 1-4103-0500-7 (paperback : alk. paper)
  ISBN 1-4103-0327-6 (hardback : alk. paper)
  1. Brachiosaurus—Juvenile literature. I. Calvetti, Leonello. II. Massini, Luca. III. Title. IV. Dalla Vecchia, Fabio Marco. Dinosaur profiles.
  QE862.S3D37 2004
  567.913—dc22
                                       2004008577

Printed in China
10 9 8 7 6 5 4 3 2 1

CONTENTS

A Changing World 6

A Giant Dinosaur 8

Brachiosaurus Babies 10

Feeding Time 12

Dry Season 14

A Dangerous World 16

The Brachiosaurus Body 18

Digging Up Brachiosaurus 20

The Largest Sauropods 22

The Evolution of Dinosaurs 24

A Dinosaur's Family Tree 26

Glossary 28

For More Information 29

About the Author 30

Index 31

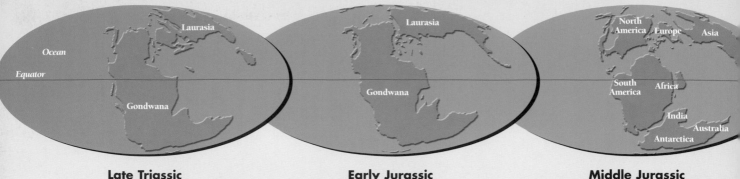

Late Triassic **227–206 million years ago**	**Early Jurassic** **206–176 million years ago**	**Middle Jurassic** **176–159 million years ago**

A Changing World

Earth's long history began 4.6 billion years ago. Dinosaurs are some of the most fascinating animals from the planet's long past.

The word *dinosaur* comes from the word dinosauria. This word was invented by the English scientist Richard Owen in 1842. It comes from two Greek words, *deinos* and *sauros*. Together, these words mean "terrifying lizards."

The dinosaur era, also called the Mesozoic era, lasted from 248 million years ago to 65 million years ago. It is divided into three periods. The first, the Triassic period, lasted 42 million years. The second, the Jurassic period, lasted 61 million years. The third, the Cretaceous period, lasted 79 million years. Dinosaurs ruled the world for a huge time span of 160 million years.

Like dinosaurs, mammals appeared at the end of the Triassic period. During the time of dinosaurs, mammals were small

Late Jurassic
159–144 million years ago

Early Cretaceous
144–99 million years ago

Late Cretaceous
99–65 million years ago

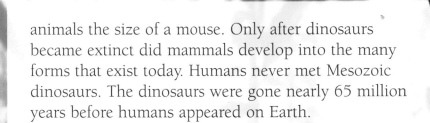

animals the size of a mouse. Only after dinosaurs became extinct did mammals develop into the many forms that exist today. Humans never met Mesozoic dinosaurs. The dinosaurs were gone nearly 65 million years before humans appeared on Earth.

Dinosaurs changed in time. *Stegosaurus* and *Brachiosaurus* no longer existed when *Tyrannosaurus* and *Triceratops* appeared 75 million years later.

The dinosaur world was different from today's world. The climate was warmer, with few extremes. The position of the continents was different. Plants were constantly changing, and grass did not even exist.

A Giant Dinosaur

Brachiosaurus belonged to the group *Sauropoda*, or saurischians. Sauropods are often called brontosaurs, which means long necks. The brachiosaur had a very long and stiff neck that made it look a little like a huge giraffe.

Sauropods were gentle plant eaters, but were so big they made the ground shake under their feet. A single brachiosaur bone or organ shows how large this dinosaur was. A rib was 9 feet (2.7 m) long. The bone of the front leg, the humerus, was more than 6 feet (2 m) long; so was the femur, or thigh bone. The scapula, or shoulder blade, was longer than the height of a man. The skull could be 31 inches (80 cm) long. A brachiosaur's huge lungs could hold more than 1,585 gallons (6,000 l) of air. Its heart weighed at least 848 pounds (385 kg).

The brachiosaur's long neck made its head look tiny compared to its huge lower body. The brachiosaur's nostrils were not at the end of its snout, as on most animals. Instead, they were on a crest between the eyes. A brachiosaur's tail was short, unlike the longer tails of similar dinosaurs such as *Diplodocus* and *Apatosaurus*.

The front legs of a brachiosaur were longer than its back legs. This made its back slope down. Other sauropods had more level backs. *Brachiosaurus* walked on all four feet. It was very slow because of its great size. Scientists think that the fastest it could move was only about 10 miles (16 km) per hour. The largest adults probably moved even more slowly.

Adult brachiosaurs probably slept standing up. They were so huge that if they settled on the ground, they would not be able to get up.

Brachiosaurus lived about 150 million years ago at the end of the Jurassic period. Scientists know of two species of *Brachiosaurus*.

One is called *Brachiosaurus altithorax*. It lived on the plains of present-day Colorado and Utah. The other is called *Brachiosaurus brancai*. It lived in present-day Tanzania, in Africa. Since *Brachiosaurus* lived in both North America and Africa, the two continents were probably connected at one time.

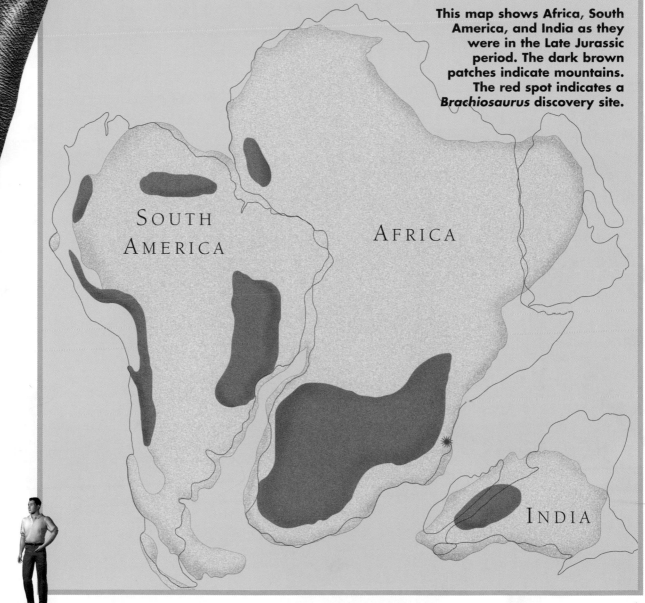

This map shows Africa, South America, and India as they were in the Late Jurassic period. The dark brown patches indicate mountains. The red spot indicates a *Brachiosaurus* discovery site.

SOUTH AMERICA

AFRICA

INDIA

BRACHIOSAURUS BABIES

Brachiosaur mothers laid large round eggs in nests in the sand. They were too large to sit on the eggs as birds do. This meant that both the hatchlings and the eggs needed protection from predators. The adults of the herd probably watched over the nests.

FEEDING TIME

Brachiosaurus could reach higher up in the trees for its food than other plant-eating dinosaurs. Its teeth were strong enough to tear off leaves and small branches. A small, young brachiosaur probably ate plants and tender shoots that grew closer to the ground.

Unlike plant-eating mammals, *Brachiosaurus* swallowed its food without chewing it. Like some plant-eating birds, it swallowed stones called gastroliths to help it digest its food.

DRY SEASON

Brachiosaurus lived on dry, coastal plains similar to the grassy African savanna. However, the plant material then was different from what grows there today. Grass did not yet exist. There were no flowering plants such as palm trees.

After the short rainy season came the long dry season. In the dry season, it was hard for a *Brachiosaurus* herd to find enough food to eat and water to drink. Finding water was important for all the dinosaurs of the plains. Usually they circled the few remaining puddles and drank side by side. Predators, especially crocodiles, would hide nearby and try to sneak up on them.

A Dangerous World

Brachiosaurus was the largest animal of its time. Predators were probably afraid to attack the huge adults. However, the young could be prey for meat-eating dinosaurs. One such predator was the quick, 20-foot (6-m) long *Elaphrosaurus*. It would approach while the herd was too busy eating to notice it. Then it would attack a helpless young dinosaur. Elaphrosaurs knew that the young brachiosaur's giant parents were too slow to stop them. Elaphrosaurs preferred to attack easier prey, though, because a fight with an adult brachiosaur could prove fatal.

THE BRACHIOSAURUS BODY

nostril

lower jaw

orbit

cervical rib

Side view of skull

scapula

cervical vertebra

The *Brachiosaurus* skeleton had some unusual features. The skull had a long snout with teeth shaped like chisels. Its cervical ribs (neck ribs) were very long and thin. This made the neck stiff. It could not bend in an S shape. The large vertebrae of the spinal column were made of thin bone that had many cavities, or holes. This helped keep the dinosaur from being too heavy.

The front legs were shaped like columns, the way an elephant's are. They rested on feet with five short toes. One toe had a short claw. This may have been used as a weapon for defense. A completely preserved back foot of *Brachiosaurus* has not yet been found. The back feet probably also had five short toes.

front foot

claw on digit 1

Dorsal view of skeleton

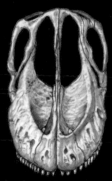

Front view of skull

A

B

A. Anterior view of skeleton (without neck and skull)

B. Posterior view of skeleton (without tail)

C. Front view of right front foot of *Brachiosaurus*

D. Right back foot of *Camarasaurus*, a sauropod relatively close to *Brachiosaurus*

C

D

dorsal vertebra

dorsal rib

femur

tibia

fibula

back foot

caudal vertebra

19

DIGGING UP BRACHIOSAURUS

Brachiosaurs were very big animals, but they are usually found in small pieces. After they died, their bodies were often ripped into pieces by scavengers. Sometimes the bodies rotted and were torn apart by rough water in rivers. Parts of the bodies then reached the bottoms of rivers and lakes. The pieces were then covered by sand. Some brachiosaur limbs have been found upright in the sand like large pillars. These animals probably died while stuck in quicksand.

The first *Brachiosaurus* skeleton was found in Colorado in 1900 by the paleontologist Elmer S. Riggs. It was incomplete and did not have a skull. In 1903, Riggs named it *Brachiosaurus* because of its long front legs. This name came from Latin and Greek words meaning "lizard-arm." The bones of a *Brachiosaurus* that Riggs studied are on display at the Field Museum in Chicago.

There are very few *Brachiosaurus* skeletons. Only a few museums have them. The most complete *Brachiosaurus* skeletons were found in the hills of Tendaguru, Tanzania, in Africa. German paleontologists began digging there between 1908 and 1912. They found five partial skeletons and three skulls.

A complete skeleton was created from these bones at the Humboldt Museum of Berlin, in Germany. At 74 feet (22.5 m) long and 39 feet (11.8 m) high, it is the largest dinosaur skeleton in the world. Its total weight is between 30 and 54 tons (27.2 and 49 metric tons). This skeleton has been on display

since 1937. It was taken apart during World War II to protect it from bombs. After the war was over, it was put back together. The Humboldt skeleton is not from a completely grown animal. Some bones found at Tendaguru belonged to even larger brachiosaurs.

Above: A *Brachiosaurus* leg bone shows how big the animal was. Left: A skeleton of *Brachiosaurus* is displayed at the Humboldt Museum in Berlin.

Places where
sauropod fossils
have been found
are noted on
the map.

THE LARGEST
SAUROPODS

Many scientists
believe that the
Chicxulub crater off
the coast of Mexico
was made by a
meteorite that led
to the extinction of
the dinosaurs.

*Amargasaurus,
Argentina,
125 million
years ago*

*Camarasaurus,
USA, 154–148
million years ago*

Sauropods lived all around the world for more than 140 million years. There were many in North America during the Late Jurassic era and in South America during the Cretaceous period, 125 to 70 million years ago. An adult sauropod was rarely less than 39 feet (12 m) long, but dwarf species lived in Europe.

- **Brachiosaurus, Tanzania and USA, 155–145 million years ago**

- **Saltasaurus, Argentina, about 75–70 million years ago**

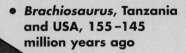

- **Diplodocus, USA, 154–148 million years ago**

THE GREAT EXTINCTION

Sixty-five million years ago, 80 million years after the time of *Brachiosaurus*, dinosaurs became extinct. This may have happened because a large meteorite struck Earth. A wide crater caused by a meteorite exactly 65 million years ago has been located along the coast of the Yucatán Peninsula in Mexico. The impact of the meteorite would have produced an enormous amount of dust. This dust would have stayed suspended in the atmosphere and blocked sunlight for a long time. A lack of sunlight would have caused a drastic drop of the earth's temperature and killed plants. The plant-eating dinosaurs would have died, starved and frozen. As a result, meat-eating dinosaurs would have had no prey and would also have starved.

Some scientists believe dinosaurs did not die out completely. They think that birds were feathered dinosaurs that survived the great extinction. That would make the present-day chicken and all of its feathered relatives descendants of the large dinosaurs.

THE EVOLUTION OF DINOSAURS

The oldest dinosaur fossils are 220–225 million years old and have been found mainly in South America. They have also been found in Africa, India, and North America. Dinosaurs probably evolved from small and nimble bipedal reptiles like the Triassic *Lagosuchus* of Argentina. Dinosaurs were able to rule the world because their legs were held directly under the body, like those of modern mammals. This made them faster and less clumsy than other reptiles.

Since 1887, dinosaurs have been divided into two groups based on the structure of their hips. Saurischian dinosaurs had hips shaped like those of modern lizards. Ornithischian dinosaurs had hips shaped like those of modern birds.

Triceratops is one of the Ornithischian dinosaurs, whose hip bones (inset) are shaped like those of modern birds.

Tyrannosaurus is in the Saurischian group of dinosaurs, whose hip bones (inset) are shaped like those of modern lizards.

There are two main groups of saurischians. One group is sauropodomorphs. This group includes sauropods, such as *Brachiosaurus*. Sauropods ate plants and were quadrupedal, meaning they walked on four legs. The other group of saurischians, theropods, includes bipedal meat-eating predators. Some paleontologists believe birds are a branch of theropod dinosaurs.

Ornithischians are all plant eaters. They are divided into three groups. Thyreophorans include the quadrupedal stegosaurians, including *Stegosaurus*, and ankylosaurians, including *Ankylosaurus*. The other two groups are ornithopods, which includes *Edmontosaurus* and marginocephalians.

A Dinosaur's Family Tree

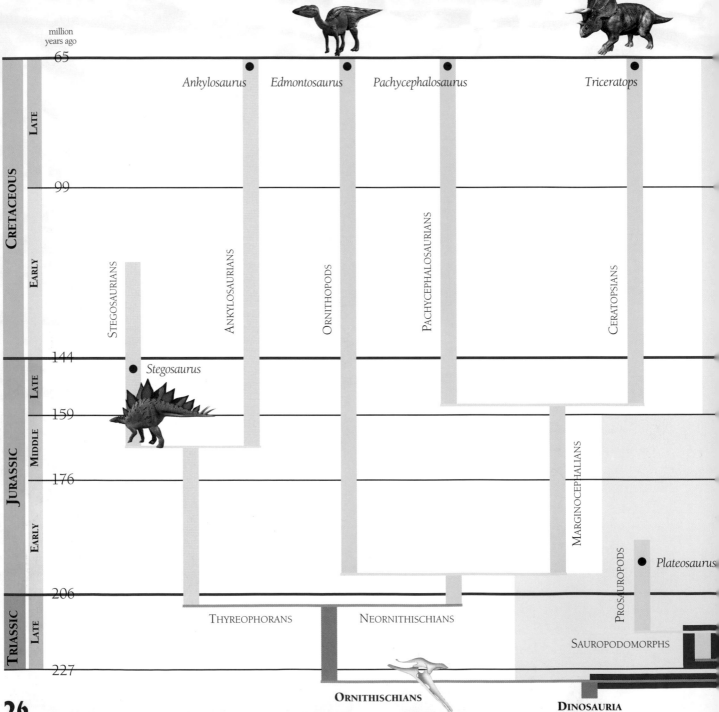

million
years ago

CRETACEOUS

LATE

65

Ankylosaurus   Edmontosaurus   Pachycephalosaurus   Triceratops

99

EARLY

STEGOSAURIANS

ANKYLOSAURIANS

ORNITHOPODS

PACHYCEPHALOSAURIANS

CERATOPSIANS

144

JURASSIC

LATE

Stegosaurus

159

MIDDLE

176

MARGINOCEPHALIANS

EARLY

PROSAUROPODS

Plateosaurus

206

TRIASSIC

LATE

THYREOPHORANS   NEORNITHISCHIANS

SAUROPODOMORPHS

227

ORNITHISCHIANS   **DINOSAURIA**

26

ORNITHOMIMOIDEANS

Ornithomimus

Tyrannosaurus

TYRANNOSAUROIDS

OVIRAPTOROSAURIANS

DEINONYCHOSAURIANS

Deinonychus

BIRDS

Scipionyx

Caudipteryx

SAUROPODS

ORNITHOLESTES

Brachiosaurus

THEROPODS

SAURISCHIANS

Glossary

Bipedal moving on two feet

Bone hard tissue made mainly of calcium phosphate

Caudal related to the tail

Cervical related to the neck

Cretaceous Period the period of geological time between 144 and 65 million years ago

Dorsal related to the back

Egg a large cell enclosed in a shell produced by reptiles and birds to reproduce themselves

Feathers outgrowth of the skin of birds and some dinosaurs, used for flight

Femur thigh bone

Fibula the outer of the two bones in the lower leg

Fossil a part of an organism of an earlier geologic age, such as a skeleton or leaf imprint, that has been preserved in the earth's crust

Jurassic Period the period of geological time between 206 and 144 million years ago

Mesozoic Era the period of geological time between 248 and 65 million years ago

Meteorite a piece of iron or rock that falls to Earth from space

Orbit the opening in the skull surrounding the eye

Paleontologist scientist who studies prehistoric life

Quadrupedal moving on four feet

Scapula shoulder blade

Scavenger animal that eats dead animals or plants

Skeleton the structure of an animal body, made up of bones

Skull the bones that form the cranium and the face

Tibia the shinbone

Triassic Period the period of geological time between 248 and 206 million years ago

Vertebrae the bones of the backbone

FOR MORE INFORMATION

Books

Paul M. Barrett, *National Geographic Dinosaurs*.
Washington, DC: National Geographic Society, 2001.

Tim Haines, *Walking with Dinosaurs: A Natural History*.
New York: Dorling Kindersley, 2000.

David Lambert, Darren Naish, and Elizabeth Wyse,
*Dinosaur Encyclopedia: From Dinosaurs to the Dawn of
Man*. New York: Dorling Kindersley, 2001.

Web Sites

The Cyberspace Museum of Natural History
www.cyberspacemuseum.com/dinohall.html
An online dinosaur museum that includes descriptions and illustrations.

Dinodata
www.dinodata.net
A site that includes detailed descriptions of fossils,
illustrations, and news about dinosaur research and
recent discoveries.

**The Smithsonian National Museum of Natural
History**
www.nmnh.si.edu/paleo/dino
A virtual tour of the Smithsonian's National Museum
of Natural History dinosaur exhibits.

About the Author

Fabio Marco Dalla Vecchia is the curator of the Paleontological Museum of Monfalcone in Gorizia, Italy. He has participated in several paleontological field works in Italy and other countries and has directed paleontological excavations in Italy. He is the author of more than fifty scientific articles that have been published in national and international journals.

INDEX

babies, 10

birds, 12, 23, 24, 25

body, 18–19, 24

bone, 8, 18, 20, 21

Brachiosaurus, 7, 23

  body, 18–19

  description, 8–9

claw, 18

Cretaceous period, 6–7, 23

danger, 16

defense, 18

digestion, 12

dinosaurs, 6–7

  family tree, 26–27

dry season, 14

eggs, 10

elaphrosaur, 16

evolution, 24

extinction, 7, 22, 23

family tree, 26–27

feet, 8, 18

food, 12, 14

fossils, 22, 24

gastroliths, 12

head, 8

heart, 8

hips, 24

humans, 7

Jurassic period, 6–7, 8, 9, 23

legs, 8, 18, 20, 21, 24

lizards, 24

lungs, 8

Index

mammals, 6–7, 24

meat eaters, 16, 25

Mesozoic era, 6, 7

meteorite, 22, 23

neck, 8, 18

nest, 10

ornithischian, 24–25, 26

plant eaters, 8, 12, 24–25

predator, 10, 14, 16, 25

quicksand, 20

reptiles, 24

rib, 8

saurischian, 8, 24–25, 27

sauropod, 8, 22–23, 25

scapula, 8

scavengers, 20

skeleton, 18, 19, 20–22

skull, 8, 18, 20

snout, 8, 18

tail, 8

teeth, 12, 18

theropods, 25

toes, 18

Triassic period, 6, 24

water, 14

weapon, 18